You are capable of AMAZING THINGS.

i hide myself within my flower
that fading from your vase
you unsuspecting feel for me
almost a loneliness

ED

Jenifer

De ort is one of the best plases to call home.........

omg so s

I love god.. HE is great. And wonderful.

-88

CALL ME

megazord

Why the hell not?

hi Th eat th g ver

People always wonder what's going t
,thistakes time away from experien
 ou
you might acomplish (accomplish)
if you doubt. peace out yo,

1. I had toshow my daugher where n
board.

I wrote two fifteen page term pape
uate paperson oneof these babies.

i
I

Do you know how loved you are?

$\frac{1}{12}$..."esoteric family language", "

NOTES from a PUBLIC TYPEWRITER

Where's the power button?

-note left on our typewriter

NOTES from a PUBLIC TYPEWRITER

edited by **MICHAEL GUSTAFSON**

and

OLIVER UBERTI

GRAND CENTRAL PUBLISHING

Grand Central Publishing
Hachette Book Group
1290 Avenue of the Americas, New York, NY 10104
grandcentralpublishing.com
twitter.com/grandcentralpub

First Edition: March 2018

Grand Central Publishing is a division of Hachette Book Group, Inc. The Grand Central Publishing name and logo is a trademark of Hachette Book Group, Inc.

The publisher is not responsible for websites (or their content) that are not owned by the publisher.

The Hachette Speakers Bureau provides a wide range of authors for speaking events. To find out more, go to *www.hachettespeakersbureau.com* or call (866) 376-6591.

Print book interior design by Oliver Uberti

Library of Congress Control Number: 2017963492

ISBN: 978-1-5387-2911-3

Printed in the United States of America

LSC-C

10 9 8 7 6 5 4 3 2 1

MICHAEL

for Hilary

OLIVER

for Sophie

CONTENTS

BOOKS
LIT
LITERATI

124
OPEN
RESTAURANT

PREFACE *by Michael Gustafson*

In the spring of 2013, my wife, Hilary, and I opened Literati Bookstore in Ann Arbor, Michigan. Opening a community-minded independent bookstore was a dream we'd shared since we bonded over books on our first date. After we got engaged, we quit our jobs in New York City, moved home to Michigan, took out a loan, and signed a lease. We were in our late twenties, pursuing a dream. We were terrified.

When opening day arrived, we unlocked the door and held our breath. One by one, people walked inside, paged through new books, discussed favorite authors. The wood floors creaked; cash registers rang. The bookstore came alive. As I stood at the register, my ears perked up. Amid the din, I heard the faint but distinct cadence of someone typing.

That morning, I had set out a typewriter on our lower level for anyone to use. It was a community-building experiment: What if people could walk into a bookstore and type anything they wanted? Would they write haikus, confessions, or declarations of love?

Would they contemplate the meaning of life? Would they make fart jokes? Would people even *know how to use* a typewriter?

The public typewriter experiment, for me, was also personal. The first typewriter I ever fell in love with was my grandfather's—a 1930s Smith Corona. Because he died when I was young, my memory of him is limited to impressions: visits to the Florida condo he shared with my grandmother, beach picnics, golf cart rides around the neighborhood, and an alluring black typewriter on his writing desk. One year, long after he passed, Grandma gave me his Smith Corona for Christmas. At the time, I was a struggling writer. Seeing his old typewriter again stirred something in me. As I hunched over the keys, I imagined my grandfather also click-clacking away, equally hunched, considering each word. His typewriter made writing *fun* again. And for the first time since his death, I felt connected to him, to a past I never really knew. Now, his typewriter is rarely far from sight; I keep it inside a glass display case below our bookstore's register.

The typewriter I set out on opening day was a light blue Olivetti Lettera 32. I inserted a clean piece of paper and let it be. There were no prompts. No directions. Just the world's smallest publishing house, waiting for an author. One of the notes I found that first day was: `Thank you for being here.` I didn't see the typer's identity, so it appeared as though the typewriter itself was thanking *me.* As though the dusty machine was happy to be used again.

Soon, more notes accumulated. People proposed, broke up, confessed, apologized, joked, and philosophized. I had to buy more paper, more ink ribbons, more typewriters. Typewriting had become part of our bookstore's identity. I taped favorite notes to a wall behind the typewriter. I shared some notes in store newsletters and on social media. And in 2015, we commissioned artist Oliver Uberti to paint fifteen of them along a 60-foot stretch of our building. It's now one of the most photographed locations in town.

Customers, friends, and family began encouraging me to turn these notes into a book. At first, I was apprehensive. But then I read through the piles of messy, typewritten pages again with Oliver. Some made us tear up; many made us laugh out loud. Our community of note-typers has shown that impactful writing isn't limited to bestselling authors. Each of us has a note to leave behind, and I realized more of them deserve to be read. They shouldn't be locked inside my filing cabinet at home. Inside our store, surrounded by books that have been labored over by authors, editors, and marketers, there's a way for people to publish directly into the world in permanent ink—spelling errors and all.

Some nights after we close, when the bookstore is quiet and the lights are dim, I'll pull from the display case my grandfather's old

Smith Corona. I'll set it on a table in the dark, where it makes a loud *thunk.* The ink still smacks one letter at a time, as it did eighty years ago.

I pause in the quietude. I wonder, like so many others have before: *What should I write?* I decide to write to the person who gave me the typewriter. The click-clack reverberates. I strike the wrong letter. My pinkie reaches for the delete key, but there isn't one. I'm glad. I keep typing.

Dear Grandpma,

This typewrite is prtty awsome

tutututuyirjfhfgh
This typewriter is cool
The seasons change but we do n

If we were a movie, you,d be

Why doesn;t autocorrect work

I wish you weren,t so self abs

Pretty sure my computer has th

If I had a dime for every time
you're not wearing pants."..

his is the most Everyone so

Jo g and Rebekah loves books

poop

I

this thing?

bed

read
god is a cat.

font.

he poop that took a pee. Chapte

omeone told me, "It looks like

.

A customer leaves a note.

TALK TYPEWRITER TO ME

Kurt Vonnegut used to say, "Write to please just one person." When it comes to our public typewriter, there is one dedicated reader.

Hi.

I know people aren't necessarily writing to please *me.* Still, I am the one who reads each typed note. Every nonsensical musing. Every spelling error. Every poem. Every bad pun. Every note questioning love. Every unquestionable `I love you.`

Over the years, I have noticed patterns of typing behavior. During Michigan football season, an Ohio State fan will type: `Go Bucks.` On a cold, snowy Saturday night, a customer hopes for a date or comments on sobriety. Come spring, graduating seniors type memories, leave behind advice for incoming freshmen, or write: `I will miss you, Ann Arbor.`

At the end of each day, I retreat to the office to make sense of this ongoing—though slightly disjointed—inked monologue.

I understand that poring over anonymously typed fragments might not be the best use of my free time, but at any moment, on any day, an unheralded (or heralded) literary genius could leave behind an astute meditation, a whimsical missive, or unprecedented poetic artistry—and I don't want to miss it. So I will eagerly leaf through pages of `,,,,,...???867()*` and `89khellohello` to find one sentence of sincerity.

Finding a great note requires a bit of detective work. Many times, notes are typed atop other notes. Picking through the layers leads to discoveries or, sometimes, more questions. `I was just robbed` was a note I read the other day. It was next to `I miss you.` I believe these notes were written separately. Then I reread them. Maybe not.

Before we set out the typewriter, I had a vision that each person who typed a note would participate in a never-ending story, picking up where the last person left off. The plot would twist and turn, the characters would come and go, and, over decades, it could become the Great American Novel—penned by America.

Now, having reviewed thousands of notes in the process of compiling this book, I am starting to view this collection more as a Great Global Diary. The notes from our public typewriter come from an anonymous and unpredictable array of voices: Locals. Tourists. Investment managers. Window washers. Christians.

Muslims. Newlyweds. Widowers. Bus drivers. Engineering students. Schoolchildren. Retirees. The scared. The lonely. The content. The brokenhearted. The beloved.

They continue to type, and I continue to read.

Rheinmetall

—

Life,
like this
typewriter,
has no
backspace.
Type strongly
and don't
look back.

—

At morning light the raven soars
to it$ perch cloaked in darrk

Watching my son try to type
a single sentence is like watching a
crocodile trying to do ballet.

—

My son thinks that
I am a genius because
I know how to type...
finally, he is
impressed with me.

Monday, August 25, 2014

With every day
school draws nearer.
I don't know whether to be excited
or nervous
or totally freaking out
or sort of okay
or kinda paranoid.
I guess middle school will be okay,
sort of

—

advice for graduates?

Don't do it!

TRAVEL • PSYCHOLOGY
HEALTH • COOKING • ART
GARDENING
WRITING

—

I'm scared I'll spend half my life deciding what to do with it and the other half regretting that choice.

Everyone has a superpower.
The trick is to find it.

hello i am very gay... ;)

—

I’m pregnant with my first child.
40 years old and I feel life is just beginning. Hello.

—

I spent 22 years telling her
to do great things. Now that she has
gone to do them I am sad.

—

I love my mommy.

—

Your mother loves you.

Babies are so small. We want some.
Maybe 7. Maybe 2. Who knows?
and part of how many we have depends
on if he wants to have that many.
He probably wants three, being
a triplet himself. The babies will
be so cute though. I can't imagine why
he wouldn't want 7 of them.

—

I was four when my dad left.
Today I met him and finally reconciled.
I love my family.

—

i ran into my stepsister here,
and my friend says if we were related
she'd be the prettier sister. She also
smells like sausage.

dear mommy everyone
I love the whole family
and I will love
all of you for ever
and I love all of your
hearts for ever.
Have great hopes for ever
I hope your days are magical
love noah.

We had a date night and
chose to come to Literati.
Please do not tell our children
we came here without them.

LITERATI
BOOKSTORE

A NEW HOME

When your logo is a typewriter, people bring you typewriters. A grandmother's forgotten heirloom. A great-uncle's college workhorse. An Underwood #5 rescued from an antique shop. Like a houseplant or automobile, a typewriter is a commitment. It requires space, attention, love. Sometimes, people run out of these.

"It was my father's," a customer says, handing me a typewriter, "but our apartment is too small."

Or: "I would toss it, but maybe you want it?"

As much as I love sheltering orphaned machines, eventually—after the accumulation of, say, thirty of them—one looks around and thinks, *I have a lot of typewriters.* But customers keep bringing in 1940s Royals, 1920s Coronas, and Underwoods. I can't say no. Even when the "k" is inoperable.

One afternoon, a woman knocked on our office door. She was carrying a large metal case.

"Is Mike in?"

The other booksellers exchanged glances. This customer, who

I'll call Anna, plunked the case down. It could be only one thing.

"Aha," I said. "A typewriter!"

I opened the case to find a 1950s seafoam-green Hermes 3000. Okay condition. Some dust and grime. I tested its keys and carriage.

"It works," Anna added, "but it could use a little care."

Anna was a fellow analogue enthusiast. She had purchased this model at a thrift store but decided she no longer wanted it. We discussed best typewriter buying practices, lamented drawbacks of buying online (shipping), and exchanged typewriter repairman rumors: She had heard of "a guy outside Detroit." I told her of a "shop near Cincinnati." Typewriters, like vinyl record players, are appreciating. Yet despite recent popularity, few people know how to fix them. They break, and remain broken.

"If we put this typewriter out, be warned: It's a death sentence," I said. "Once a typewriter goes public, it's got six months."

I showed her our beautiful ruins—typewriters maligned by public use. They get knocked over; carriages malfunction; hammers bend. Many customers type too fast. The keys jam. In an attempt to fix those keys, a type-bar link detaches. "I think the typewriter's broken," customers tell me. I show them how to adjust line spacing, work the feed roller, and operate the carriage return. Still, I know all public typewriters will break eventually. When they do, we set some in our store window overlooking the sidewalk. The Boulevard of Broken Typewriters. It's a nice view, at least.

As Anna browsed our Boulevard, I spotted an Underwood once donated by a couple in their mid-50s. I remember being reluctant to accept the broken machine. "This was our mother's, whose life was books," they said when they dropped it off. "We'd love if it had a nice home." Years later, they saw their mom's Underwood in our window, warmly lit, surrounded by books. "It's like she's still here," they said. Once someone tells you that, the typewriter stays. Broken or not.

I turned to Anna. "I make no promises this typewriter will have such a view," I said, gesturing toward the Boulevard, to pedestrians and the snowy sidewalk beyond. "But I'll try to give it a nice home."

"Do what you'd like," Anna said. "I'm not emotionally attached."

I was relieved. One less typewriter to worry about breaking. But I was also disappointed. In their past lives, typewriters in our store were *used*—for term papers, wedding invitations, letters to representatives, funeral announcements. The scope of a person's life, typed on one machine. To me, that deserves emotional attachment.

After Anna left, I sat with her green Hermes. I touched a key. Then another. With each click-clack, the dust and grime wore off, its keys and hammers rediscovering their rhythm. Like a forgotten record player spinning new songs, Anna's typewriter whistled, popped, and played into the night.

—

I don’t know what to say.

—

permanent ink holds my hands back.

—

I love typewriters because
I can type aggressively.

—

I just want to
push your buttons.

—

Why does this thing
have a hashtag symbol?
They didn't have Twitter.
#weird

—

what is the password?

—

Avoid identity theft. Use a typewriter.
They are much harder to hack.

FADE IN:

INT. Bookstore-Day

MAN

How did people write movies on this?

FADE TO BLACK

The trick is to make sure all letters
are uniform in their appearance.
If you can type a “q” or “z” with the
same force as a “t” or “e,” then you
are doing pretty well.

If I had to write a
five-paragraph essay on
this thing, I would withdraw
from middle school.

—

Before spellcheck, there was spelling.

—

Misspelling is a suign of genius.

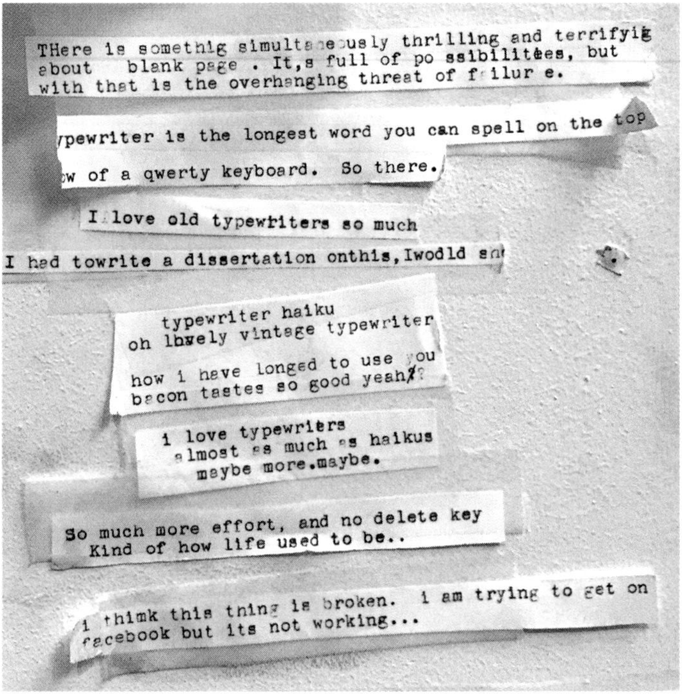

THere is somethig simulta e usly thrilling and terrifyig
about blank page . It,s full of po ssibilitees, but
with that is the overhanging threat of f ilur e.
ypewriter is the longest word you can spell on the top
w of a qwerty keyboard. So there.
I love old typewriters so much
I had towrite a dissertation onthis,Iwodld
typewriter haiku
oh lovely vintage typewriter
how i have longed to use you
bacon tastes so good yeah?
i love typewriters
almost as much as haikus
maybe more.maybe.
So much more effort, and no delete key
Kind of how life used to be..
i thimk this thing is broken. i am trying to get on
facebook but its not working...

The Wall of Fame

—

Fame is a social construct.
Screw your wall.

—

In person you can pretend,
but in writing
everything shows as
it is meant to be.

—

enveloped in an envelope,
these words would do no good.
they might sit for centuries
in a PO Box
or in a box you open only
when the leaves lose their
last hint of green and
sit perplexed on your office floor
where you've let the stacks
stack up

and think how glad you are
to get to read them at all.

nostalgia is overrated
please be gentle with me. I'm old.
ROYAL

—

Typewriters remind us
that words are sound--
they make noise
like the striking of keys
the scratch of pen on paper.

What have we lost now that
words are silent?

State Street, 1955

WAHRS
BOOKS
QUARRY
STATIONERY
MORRILL
TYPEWRITERS
MORRILL'S
OFFICE FURNITURE
Display Rooms Second Floor
FOUNTAIN PENS
314
MORRILL'S
314
Gifts Chester Roberts Gifts

CITY OF BOOKS

While on the Ann Arbor District Library's website, I came upon a collection of historic photographs of the city. One image, in particular, caught my eye: State Street, in 1955, from the roof of the old Wagner's clothing store, a few doors down from the State Theater. The University of Michigan campus hides just out of frame. Among the historic buildings, I saw neon signs and hand-painted awnings, Oldsmobiles and fedora hats. Zooming in, I found three signs that read BOOKS and a typewriter shop. A book lover's paradise.

I printed this photo and taped it on my wall.

Ann Arbor has a rich bookselling past. Sixteen years after this photo was taken, the original Borders bookstore opened around the corner in 1971. According to the *Ann Arbor News*, Tom and Louis Borders "received advice not to open a bookstore in Ann Arbor since at that time one store had closed and several others were on the verge of it."

Before we opened Literati in 2013, Hilary and I received the same advice. Borders had just sold its last book in 2011, and before that, Shaman Drum, another beloved independent bookstore, closed in 2009. Some close to us said we were crazy. Some called it professional suicide. "How can *you* survive if Borders couldn't?" a landlord asked. He rejected our lease bid and hung up the telephone.

It was a tough time for bookstores nationwide, and the struggle was well documented. CNN profiled Borders' last days with an article titled "The death and life of a great American bookstore." I remember reading this same article while living in Brooklyn with Hilary. We both grew up in Michigan. Hilary browsed the Ann Arbor Borders' bookshelves as a kid. I remember feeling both sorrowful and motivated and thinking how a well-read university town like Ann Arbor needed a vibrant, downtown independent bookstore.

A few months later, newly engaged, we began working on a business plan.

When we moved back to Michigan, we were told that at one point Ann Arbor had the most bookstores per capita of any US city. The city still supports ten indies, but there are fewer now than thirty years ago. Before we opened, people told us they were afraid bookstores would disappear forever, perhaps the same thing the Borders brothers were told decades earlier: "I thought Ann Arbor would never get another bookstore!" or "I'm so happy a bookstore is actually *opening*."

Literati Bookstore exists because great bookstores existed before us. Our inventory sits on shelves repurposed from that same original Borders store where Hilary once browsed. Two booksellers profiled in CNN's eulogy are now Literati booksellers. And in 2015, we were featured in a *new* article, "The Return of the Great American Indie Bookstore." A flattering statement, but it made me wonder: *If bookstores return, where do they return from?*

When a bookstore closes, it does not die and disappear. A bookstore reincarnates. The ideas contained in the bookstores from that old 1955 Ann Arbor photograph—Slater's, Follett's, Wahr's—have reemerged in new locations with new names. Not just in Ann Arbor, but across the country wherever entrepreneurs are inspired by bookstores of the past. Like a dormant perennial, a bookstore will sprout again.

One day (far in the future, I hope), Literati's season, too, will end. While it exists, each week, I climb to the top of the parking garage across the street from our bookstore and photograph a bookstore in bloom. Then I turn these photos into postcards and post them on social media. I hope that, forty years from now, a potential bookstore proprietor will not be deterred by articles, churlish landlords, and pundits predicting "the end of books."

Instead, I hope that person stumbles upon old photographs of Ann Arbor. I hope she sees a busy downtown street. I hope she squints and sees hand lettering that reads BOOKSTORE. I hope she sees books and typewriters in the windows—a warm, inviting display—and an open door that leads to hand-painted floors and handwritten recommendations, to all that ink printed on those thousands of pages, a room of ideas waiting to be rediscovered, all over again.

Washington Street, 2016

—

A bookstore
 is larger than
the universe.

 After all,
   the universe
only contains
         what IS.

—

Maybe we were brought here
to explore other worlds.
Reading allows us to do so.

—

i don’t even read books
why am i here?

—

Well-loved books always
look the most unkempt.
This does not seem to be
true of people.

—

Maybe one day we will write
enough books and read enough words
to understand each other.

I hope.

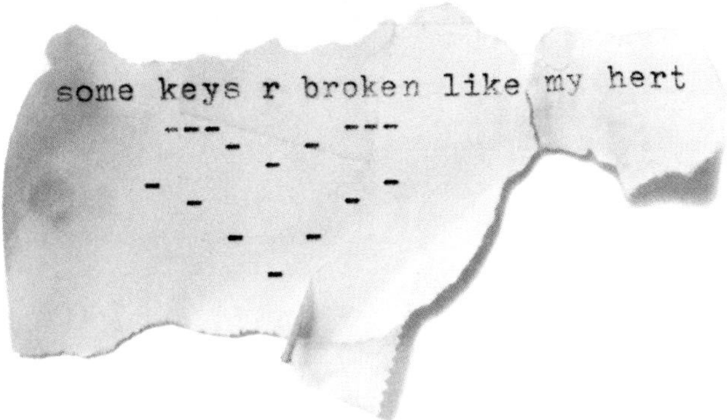
some keys r broken like my hert

IMPRESSIONS

I'll never forget the day a customer came up to me and said, "I had a dream about your typewriter."

She rolled up her left sleeve. "In my dream, I walked downstairs and saw *this*."

On her arm, in permanent 72-point Courier, was a tattoo of a word.

"My parents disapproved of me getting a tattoo," she continued. "I waited until they passed away." It was a busy Saturday night in the shop, but, honestly, how often does a woman tell you about a dream she once had about your typewriter? I set down the stack of books I was holding and talked with her more. "I wanted a word and a punctuation," she said. "Once I saw this word in my dream, I knew."

I asked to reenact her dream. So she walked downstairs to the typewriter and sat down. I fetched a new sheet of paper. Then we typed: `love.`

"Yep, that's exactly how I saw it!" she said. She extended her arm and the fresh tattoo, and I snapped a photograph of the two inked words together—one on flesh, one on paper.

"Do you want to keep this typewriter?" I asked.

"No, no. I've got my tattoo," she said, unrolling her sleeve.

I figured that anyone who dreams of typewritten letters and permanently inscribes them on her arm deserves to keep the typewriter of her dreams, so I asked again, just to be sure.

"Let someone else enjoy it," she said. "It's already left an impression on me."

love.
love.
Q W E R T Y U I O P

—

7 billion
people in
the world
and I have
the fortune
of meeting
you.

—

best date in years starting
in this bookstore

—

i am on a date
my bladder is leaking

—

quiero amarte como nadie puede amarte.
como un arbol se necicite la luz,
como el flor se necicite agua,
como el mar necicite la tierra,
nunca sufficie para describir
el manera en que me aflictas.

I want to love you like no one else can love you.
like a tree needs light,
like a flower needs water,
like a beach needs sand,
there are not enough words to describe
the way you burden me.

—

your eyes are like wonderful
august skie s

—

i love it when you talk typewriter to me

—

I remember the first time
you said you wanted to kiss me.

—

cool air, long walk. warm hand.

—

I walked in expecting
to fall in love with books,
not the person
I walked in with.

—

when was the last time someone
told you you are enough?

—

I am finally ready to let her love
all of me

—

I met the man of my dreams...
and I'm moving a thousand miles
away from him tomorrow.

—

i know i'm leaving
but i will never leave you

Oliver types with paint, June 2015.

THE TYPEWRITING ON THE WALL

Murals are usually pictures. When Oliver, the designer behind our typewriter sign, came to us with a sketch for the side of our bookstore, he had an unusual idea. He wanted to share words written *by* the community *with* the community. First, he digitized the exact font from my grandfather's Smith Corona—smudgy e's, q's, and all. Then he made a scale model of our brick wall and arranged fifteen of our favorite notes in staggered rows. After months of planning, Oliver was ready to paint. But before he could start on the lettering, he had to tape off the selected bricks and prime them white.

"People kept asking what the white bricks were," he recalls. "I said, 'Come back in a few days,' but that only stoked curiosity. More than one person looked at the white rows and said, 'Oh, I know. Pixels!'"

For a bookseller, this word-painting process was a joy to watch. "This used to be sixty feet of nothing," Oliver says. "People walked by every day, heads aimed straight ahead or down at their phones. Now those heads turn. You can't *not* read words." As you'll see on the following pages, those words are now worth a thousand pictures.

love with books,
your eyes are
I've been gay, and I've been
the last time someone told you that you
wonderful august,
What
My mom used to be a mime. I just found out.
anthropes, irony, and ellipses...
...and li
scared I'll spend half my life deciding what to do
I know who I'm going to marry.
and they're both over-rated.
I walked in expecting to fall in love with books, not the person I walked in with.
than the universe. After
love.
larger than the universe
love.

love.

This is my favorite corner in Ann Arbor.

I will find someone someday.

I know who I'm going to marry.

I know who I'm going to marry.

I will find someone someday.

This is my favorite corner in Ann Arbor.

I've been gay, and I've been straight, and they're both over-rated.

This is my favorite corner in Ann Arbor.

I will find someone someday.

your
wonderful august skie s
I know who I'm going to marry.
both over-rated.
when was the

FOUR WORDS

Over the years, our typewriters have typed thousands of words. One-liners. Poems. Paragraph-long monologues. Some make us laugh; others make us think. Some, smashed together, make no sense. Yet every now and then, a customer will walk into the store and type four words followed by a question mark. Four words that can change a life. (Or, more accurately, two.)

It was a classic autumn evening in Ann Arbor: Crimson and gold leaves fluttered onto the sidewalk. Hand in hand, he guided her into the bookstore. He looked my way. I pressed "Play" on a cued-up iPod, and their song began to fill the store. He was smiling. She was smiling. Together, they browsed, then walked downstairs.

Soon, I heard crying.

When the tears of joy had subsided, when friends and parents had emerged from their hiding spots, when the laughter and happy echoes had been absorbed into the bookshelves and everyone wandered outside, I closed up the store for the night. I ran downstairs and there, on the typewriter, were those four words:

`will u marry me?`

The happy couple was gone. I didn't want this piece of paper to be thrown out with the morning trash and lost, so I put it in a folder and took it home. A few weeks later, I contacted the bride-to-be and gave her those special words to surprise her fiancé on Christmas morning. I felt silly doing it. Maybe that's not an ideal gift—four words from a bookstore typewriter—but they didn't belong anywhere else. And I wasn't going to be the one to throw them away.

I know who I'm going to marry.

There is something

simultaneously thrilling

and terrifying

about a blank page.

It's full of possibilities,

but with that is

the overhanging threat

of failure.

A PIECE OF PAPER

Once, a man ran up to me at our cash register and said, "There's no paper in the typewriter!" He wanted to type a proposal and slip it in his girlfriend's menu at a restaurant down the street.

I handed him a piece of paper.

He walked downstairs, typed, and left.

He never came back.

We now train our booksellers to keep the typewriter paper replenished.

—

In my much longer days, I knew
a girl named J–. Unbeknownst to her,
she was the great love of my life.
My fear of her rejection is what
prevented me to tell her exactly
how I felt, and because of that fear
I sit here this day a bitter and broken
man knowing that the great love of
my life belongs to another.

—

I'm the
best book ever
written.
And most of
the people
I've loved
just can't
read.

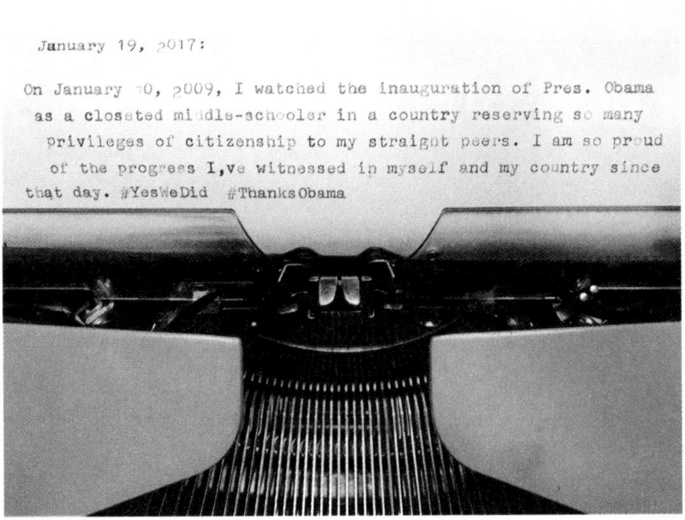
January 19, 2017:
On January 20, 2009, I watched the inauguration of Pres. Obama
as a closeted middle-schooler in a country reserving so many
privileges of citizenship to my straight peers. I am so proud
of the progress I,ve witnessed in myself and my country since
that day. #YesWeDid #ThanksObama

—

just because someone loves differently
does not mean they love less

—

There are many different types
Perhaps we love all of those types

—

i hte to do this to you
but i cnt mrry you.

—

I got a divorce this morning.
If you need me,
I'll be being single
somewhere.

—

I ended up alone on my birthday, but
being here makes it easy to forget that.
Thank you.

—

I thought it was you
I always thought it was you
For years
But it was me
It was me all along
I'll take the blame

—

I had a dream about you last night.
We were sitting on the dock at
Sun Lake like we used to in high school.
You brought your guitar and sang
shitty Tenacious D songs. You knew
I hated that band. But I let it slide
because you had that cute freckle by
your nose. And your teeth were just the
perfect kind of crooked. I still love
you, wherever you are.

—

I will find someone someday.

—

i keep realizing what i am not:
not a doctor,
not straight,
not even beloved,
but each time i get closer
to realizing who i am. and so
all these are happy negatives.

—

I am a typewriter in the streets
but a laptop in the sheets.

—

I've been gay,
and I've been
straight,
and they're
both
overrated.

MONSTER
1775
THE HOUR
PERIL

THE VIOLIN MONSTER

Our public typewriter connects all kinds: grandparents with grandchildren, people proposing, people typing knock-knock jokes. One autumn, the typewriter facilitated what may be the world's first penpalship between a seven-year-old and a werewolf.

I had seen this werewolf on the streets of Ann Arbor. Bedecked in a vest, top hat, and long black cape, he stood on street corners and played violin to gathering crowds. If you tipped him, he would howl a gleeful "AWWWWOOOOOOO!" He soon became a local celebrity known as the Violin Monster. One day, I saw the Violin Monster browsing books (the nature section, obviously). Before he left, he typed his howl and signed his name.

We tape favorite notes on the wall next to our typewriter. Some document the struggles of school; others muse about Ann Arbor, technology, or the typewriter itself. But this note authored by our town's lupine musician deserved more prominent real estate. So I taped it next to the typewriter itself, official evidence that we'd been visited by the local monster.

A few days later, a young customer saw the Violin Monster's note. To my surprise, he typed a message:

```
dear violen monster, next week could you come to
the farmers market? love Logan age 7
```

When I saw this sweet child writing to a werewolf, I wasn't sure what to do. Should I track down the Violin Monster before Logan waited at the farmers' market? The Violin Monster was an enigma. Sometimes he was on street corners, sometimes not. How do you summon a violin-playing werewolf?

I uploaded Logan's note to our Facebook page. The next day, the Violin Monster returned to the store and wrote back:

```
dear Logan, this week i'll be at the renaissance fair.
next week, I'll be at the market. hope to see you.
love Violin Monster
```

The two corresponded for the next several weeks. I shared their exchange online so the rest of us could follow along:

```
where are you going to be on Halloween violen monster?
love logan   PS I want to be you for halloween
I love your violen MUSIC
```

On Halloween, Logan visited the bookstore dressed as a mini Violin Monster. He carried a mini violin and within his fearsome mask let out a mini howl.

A few years later, I bumped into the Violin Monster at our bookstore's café. He said that he and Logan have become friends. And now, Logan is learning to play violin.

DOG

—

I wrote a letter to Santa
today so he doesn't think
we only talk to him
when we want something.

—

She wanted someone to hunt faeries with.
A real romantic who would understand
her need to look through rose-colored
glasses. She needed that, her adventurer,
the one who would tell her it was ok
if songs made her cry and the idea of
growing old was the most terrifying
thought she could think of. Someone who
would stay young of mind, at least.
Perhaps she would look back and laugh
at those naive days, that year before
twenty, but she prayed to some higher
power that she never became a true cynic.

The faeries existed. They were those timeless moments and she never wanted to become blind to their flightpaths. Maybe she was just some silly girl, writing too much on an old typewriter in a bookstore, for, perhaps, one or two people to see, but the blessing of the young is a fantastically self-centered worldview, and to her, these silly musings were the most important things to ever grace a piece of paper. But, as the paper came to an end, she could not find it worth two, perhaps growing up in a moment.

—

When we were younger,
we would color our skies purple,
our trees blue,
and it always looked perfect to us.

—

I raced the snowflakes
to see who would fall first.

My mom
used to be
a mime.
I just
found out.

She never
mentioned it.

fart fart fa rt fa rt fart fart fart
Rheinmetall
Q
W
E
R
T
Y
U
I
O
P

Forgive.

CATHARSIS

The most poignant notes are found on rainy Saturday nights. Notes on sobriety. Notes on divorce. Notes on loneliness. I don't judge; I replenish the paper.

Legendary sportswriter Red Smith was once asked how he churned out a column every single day. His response gets to the heart of writing: "You simply sit down at the typewriter, open your veins, and bleed."

It may sound maudlin, but a blank page can be cathartic. A blank page can absorb. And inside a quiet bookstore in Ann Arbor, anyone can sit down at our typewriter and scream.

—

Dear--, I love you and I hope
one day we can talk about things
when we are sober.

—

The hardest thing about
loving someone so broken
is you might fall to pieces
yourself.

—

(two days sober)
thrilled about the first
terrified of the second
do not have enough $$$
to buy a book
(today)
but I am comfortable here.
thank you.

—

Sometimes I get lost
just to assure myself someone
cares enough to find me.

—

she needs help.
I really want to help her.
But I don't know how.

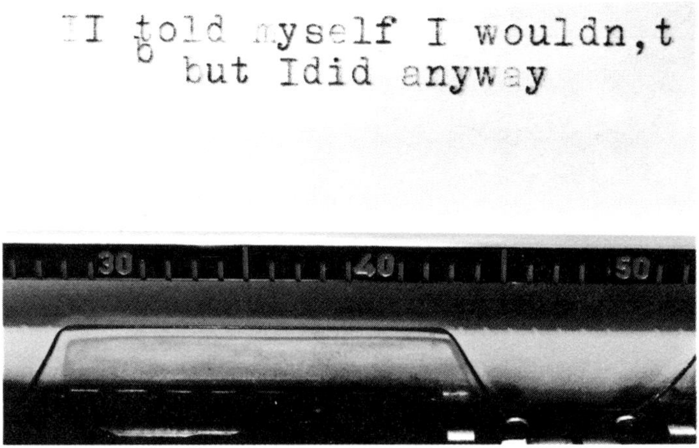
II told myself I wouldn,t
but Idid anyway
30
40
50

—

I am 7 months sober today.
I'm finally learning
how to forgive. Not only those
who hurt me, but myself.

—

i worry that my pain is not profound.

—

you know i'm scared of heights
because i'm afraid i'll jump

—

Life insists that we endure.

—

last semester I wanted to commit suicide.
But now I am in a much better place...

—

Be nice to everyone...
for we're all walking around
with unknown issues.

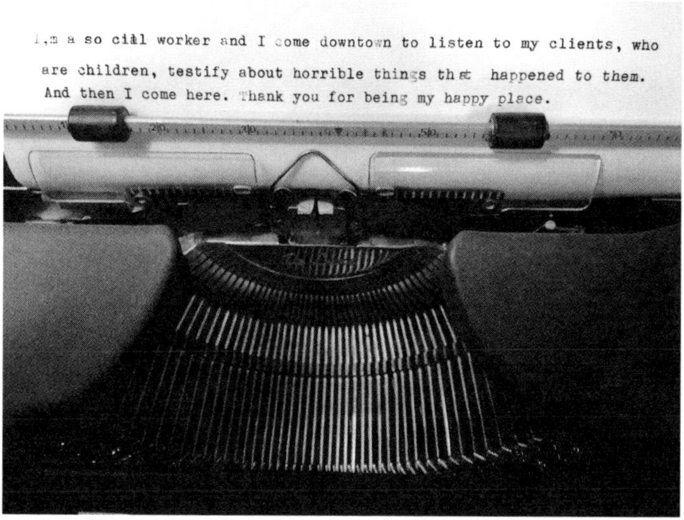
I,m a so cial worker and I come downtown to listen to my clients, who
are children, testify about horrible things th at happened to them.
And then I come here. Thank you for being my happy place.

MYSTERY
ESSAYS
THE SUN IS ALSO A STAR
THE BLACK WITCH
KIMBERLY McCREIGHT

ON MYSTERY

At night, when the customers have left and the lights are dim, I often find myself alone in our basement office. I analyze sales, tidy books, and shut down computers. The bookshelves exhale after a busy day. Everything is quiet. But some nights, upstairs, I'll hear footsteps.

"Hilary?" I call out and walk up, expecting to see my wife shelving or a bookseller packing up for the evening . . . but no one's there. Only books and shadows.

I lock the door. I turn off the lights. I check every dark corner, stairwell, closet, and bathroom. I say goodnight to the books. For a brief moment, standing in the dark, ears craned toward the walls, I hear the building's history. Who worked here. Who breathed here.

Our bookstore is a three-story historic building, constructed in 1904. Before we moved in, the building was an insurance company. In the mid-1970s, it was a left-wing bookstore and publishing house. Before that, a bakery. Once, a woman walked in and said, "I lived here." In 1947, she immigrated to Ann Arbor from postwar

Poland. Her family lived on the top floor, splitting the space with her uncle's sign company. "My pet kitty would perch here," she told me, pointing to a window in our café. "Our family's Christmas tree was there," she said, pointing to the bay window, where we now shelve children's books.

On my way back downstairs and through the basement, I stop in my tracks. There's a new note on the typewriter: `you are loved.` *Wait, when was the last person downstairs? Did I see this note while locking up?* I half-expect a coworker to leap out of the mechanical room and yell, "Surprise!" But no one's around. Just the books.

Ask any bookseller who has ever been the last person to leave a bookstore: Mystery doesn't stay in the mystery section. Despite best efforts to tidy, strange things happen. Books shelved moments ago are suddenly on the floor. Boards creaks upstairs, but only books await. A note appears on the typewriter even though you swear—*you swear*—no customer has been in the store for twenty minutes. It feels as though the words seeped from the shelves, leaked through the walls and floorboards, and splashed onto the typewriter's page. Or just possibly, the typewriter itself had something to say.

Our typewriter notes are written by all kinds of people.

A few are ghostwritten.

you
you are loved.

—

bell peppers with fig jam
are better than expected.
don't be scared.

—

Next time you are driving
on a bridge or flying on a plane
remember that it was built by
the lowest bidder

—

I am always wondering,
"Will there be lesbians?"

More often than not,
the answer is a disappointing "No"

—

I am a questionable subject
for a painting.

—

there are so many birds

—

I never trust bartenders who don't drink
or nurses who don't cough.

—

Nobody can tell me that
I can't like dolls.

—

I dislike people, misanthropes,
irony, and ellipses...

...and lists too.

Dear Max,

You were a good old cat. I’m sorry I pushed you off the couch sometimes when you wanted to sit in my lap and I was touched out from the babies and my eyes were itching. I’m sorry for the time I cut your skin by accident trying to cut out the mats and didn’t realize how bad it was at first. I’m sorry I sometimes let your nails get too long or ran out of wet food and that I let you go an extra day without your sub-Q fluids at the end. There were a lot of opportunities to not take perfect care of you as I had intended, but I hope you felt that those were the rare exception in the six years you were with us. I had a great day with you yesterday and hope you enjoyed some of your favorite things on your last day. It will always be a special memory for me. Please know you were loved and I/we will always remember you.

Love,

Your human mama

LOST & FOUND

In the summer of 2016, my grandmother turned 100 years old. To celebrate the century, my family gathered at her apartment. We spoke of lost relatives, relived memories, and browsed her collection of old photographs and letters. In her photo albums, each handwritten caption was a connection to a distant past. There was even a letter my grandfather had typed on his college typewriter—the same Smith Corona on display in our bookstore.

I, too, save letters and photos. Over the years, I've saved objects from my grandparents: a fireman's hose nozzle from the Detroit Fire Department; a lawn bowling trophy from 1984; a leather-bound collection of 1920s classic books; an original watercolor of a small house overlooking an autumn field. I display these objects around my house: on a bookshelf, above the piano, over the fireplace. Surrounded by them, I feel connected to my grandparents' lives. I glimpse who they were. What they did. How they lived.

When I type on my grandfather's Smith Corona, I listen between the click-clacks and try to remember him. His face. I remember that sunny afternoon in Florida when he looked into my nine-year-old eyes and said seriously, in the way grandfathers sometimes do, "You are very special." With enough concentration, I can remember his voice's resonance, its unique intonation. But as I get older, remembering gets harder. I type; I listen.

One day at the bookstore, I saw a new object beside my grandfather's typewriter: a small plastic ruler. The ruler itself was nothing special. Just a simple, everyday tool of measurement. But a name was printed on this one: "Ernest Gustafson."

"I found it at an antique store," said our manager, Jeanne. "It had your last name, which I thought was neat."

Then I told her my grandfather's first name was also Ernest.

She had no idea.

Somehow, this ruler once owned by an Ernest Gustafson had made its way to a typewriter once owned by our Ernest Gustafson. Suddenly, touching the ruler, I remembered that afternoon with my grandfather. *"You are very special."*

Maybe you are across an ocean, sitting in a small house overlooking a field, reading this book. Maybe you, too, have lost a grandfather. Or a cat. I imagine you sitting there, holding this book, reading words once typed thousands of miles away: `It will always be a special memory for me. Please know you were loved and that I/we will always remember you.`

Ernest Gustafson
BERG HATS
ST. LOUIS

In loving memory of
my older daughter Rachel,
who died of cancer
at age 26, a year before
this store opened.
I would get her lots of
cookbooks, but...

I can't.

—

cancer sucks

—

I feel you here
you live in books
I miss you, mom

—

mother, when they buried you--
they buried me too

Dear Nana,
You would have loved this place.
10
30

—

I fell in love with a boy
between the pages
of this basement.
Today, he's gone,
but the pages are still here.
and so am I.
and somehow,
that is enough.

—

we are all stories in the end

LAST WORD

Before I leave for home, I turn off the bookstore lights. The store is dark, but I feel comforted among the words, the pages and ink, the thousands of voices. The books hum.

As I head out the door, I notice a light on in the basement, the lamp beside our typewriter. I walk downstairs, and atop the typewriter, in full luminescence, is a single white page.

I could sit down and type. I could write about love. Or loss. Or mystery. Or about my day. I could write to my grandmother.

Tonight, I leave it blank. Tomorrow, another customer—someone having a bad day, beginning a new life, about to propose, or wanting forgiveness—will walk downstairs and, perhaps for the first time, press a finger to a typewriter key.

Snap. Click. Clack.

Words will appear on that blank page. Words that cannot evaporate. Words that will stay. Words that will stick around and bring comfort, like the books on our shelves. That's the thing about ink . . . in all its messy, smudgy, imperfect beauty. Ink lasts.

nhnen i re ch th e e
what shall come to our minds,

e ulzel,repunzel,throw down so

art thou???// Im to.ld tha
er. true story. peace out sewi
jhg

me

I will find someone some day.
*Yes , youwill! !

What are you allowed to wear w

jgn u j ,moldry hujkmgrcv

k
nbm m u 3y

i write. i write: i write. i

d of t his p eaper , wwhat will
/

e si k beats

hello
good advic is ha d tofined.
; a wow, weird typing shit ther

u

th light pink?????????

dxckg k.v.gwyi6l acbtg592 kfd h

write that i write.

$\frac{3}{4}\frac{3}{4}$

ACKNOWLEDGMENTS

It takes a community to support an independent bookstore. This book would not be possible without our community of book lovers in Ann Arbor and across the world.

In particular, we would like thank: Philip and Erin Stead for encouraging this book from the start—and for telling Oliver we needed a sign; the Violin Monster for his wonderful violin music; Tom Beauvais, for the beautiful typewriters; and Lisa Gottlieb, plus those whose photos enriched this text.

Literati Bookstore would not have sprouted without our families. Thank you, Frank Welchner; may your generosity live on. To my inspiring 101-year-old grandmother, Fran: Thank you for the Smith Corona and all those M&M's. I agree: Chocolate *is* the secret of life. Thank you to the Weimerts, Wevers, Bosserds, and Fosters; thank you, John and Kim Lowe, Kathryn and Andy Collins, Sheree Myers, and Ryan Bathie for your love and support. To my father, Peter; mother, Virginia; and sister, Lindsay: Thank you for your guidance, humor, love, and encouragement. (Helan går!) And to Hilary:

Thank you for your vision, passion, and commitment to books and literature. You are why this bookstore blooms.

To our incredible staff at Literati: Thank you for your work ethic, expertise, and heart. (And for keeping the typewriter paper replenished.)

Oliver and I also wish to thank our agents, George Lucas and Luigi Bonomi, for believing in us from day one. At Grand Central, the enthusiasm of our editor, Suzanne O'Neill, brought this book to life.

Finally, to all the people who sat at our typewriter with something to say: Thank you for participating in this project. Thank you for believing in bookstores and the power of the written word. And, in the words of one of our first typewriter notes:

Thank you for being here.

PHOTO CREDITS

pp.3,12-13,42,54,65,73,82,96,106,118,124,129,130,133,143,147,150,160: Michael Gustafson

20,30: Dodge & Burn Photography

24: Cat Buswell

58: Elisabeth Blake

60-61: Courtesy of the *Ann Arbor News*

70: Oliver Uberti

84: (Left to right, from top) Kya Liann; Dana Kilroy; Michael Gustafson; ibid.; Oliver Uberti; Rachel Clark; Allyson Miko; Kimberly Pais; Oliver Uberti; Jody Liu; Ibrahim Ijaz; Stephen Ackeret and Julie Meade

85: (Left to right, from top) Karisa Sharon; Derek R. Bridges; Natasha and Meghal Janardan; Victoria Marchenko and Franklyn Rutkowski; Katherine Robbins; Brittney Bautista; Michael Gustafson; Wendy Guo; Heather Miller; Carrie Dudewicz; Sophia Kruz; Yue Chen

86: Nicole Haley Photography

87: Jennifer Chuang

88: Edward Mauer / Edward John Photography

91: Jennifer Gaber

109: Brandon McNaughton

110: Stefanie Horvath

116: Sophia Kruz

117: Laura Meyer

ABOUT THE EDITORS

Michael Gustafson is the co-owner of Literati Bookstore, an independent bookstore in Ann Arbor, Michigan. He lives in Ann Arbor with his wife and Literati Bookstore co-owner, Hilary.

Oliver Uberti is a graphic designer and co-author of two award-winning books of maps and graphics, *Where the Animals Go* and *London: The Information Capital*. Previously, he was a senior design editor at *National Geographic*. He lives in Los Angeles.

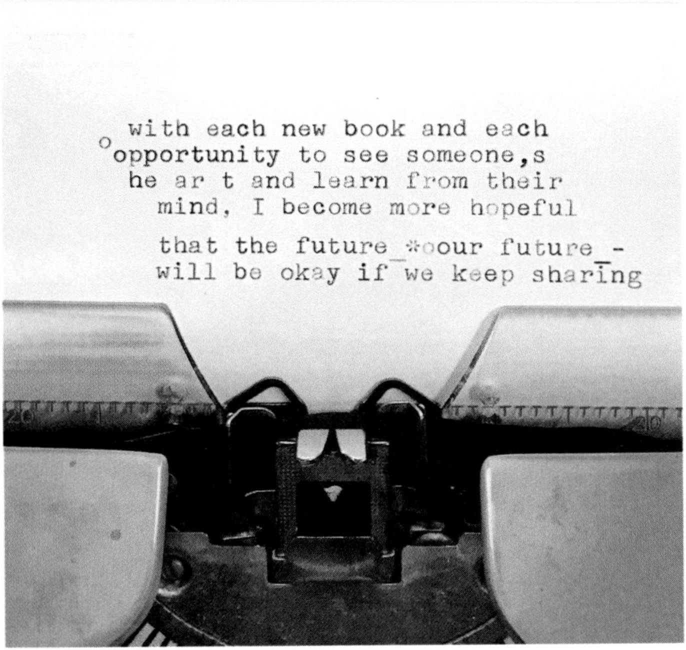
with each new book and each
opportunity to see someone,s
he ar t and learn from their
mind, I become more hopeful
that the future_*oour future_ -
will be okay if we keep sharing

ast the typewriter

just you and me and ourx

it i s a never ending ci r ll

darkness and there can only b e darkn

just you and me and our world ofxx lovean

Lincoln is waiting at home.

our kitchen don,t even know it,s the weekend

just yo u and me and

is i workin ?

just you and me and our worldx of love

audrey

is it working?

trip?

jj just you and me and me

jud the judgement cat

given right

res on your pillow

zoe ,

,k

just you and me and our nerdy little world

have they done to you

hell

zoes las

The poop that took a pee. Chapteer One

Pretty sure my computer has this font.

god is a cat.
read

h you weren,t so self absorbed

doesn;t autocorrect work on this thing?

I knwondeguyhyhivdonevyerkneew to talk

we were a movie, you,d be

poop

seasons change but we do not

typewriter is cool

Jo g and Rebekah loves books

Everyone so this is the most

y

This typewrite is prtty awsome

Every one should love bbooks!!!

Rebekah loves books!!!iwy memory in ann arbor hhh

r R e oll washere . neveerv was good at this thing. Whe re